Burned Out?

....

Trusting God with Your "To Do" List

Winston T. Smith

New
Growth
Press

www.newgrowthpress.com

New Growth Press, Greensboro, NC 27404
Copyright © 2006, 2010 by Winston T. Smith
Originally published in 2006 as *Rest.*
All rights reserved. Published 2010.

Typesetting: Robin Black, www.blackbirdcreative.biz

ISBN-10: 1-935273-20-5
ISBN-13: 978-1-935273-20-2

Library of Congress Cataloging-in-Publication Data

Smith, Winston T., 1966-
    Burned out? : trusting God with your to-do list /
Winston T. Smith.
        p. cm.
    Includes bibliographical references and index.
    ISBN-13: 978-1-935273-20-2 (alk. paper)
    ISBN-10: 1-935273-20-5 (alk. paper)
1. Burn out (Psychology)—Religious aspects—Christianity.
2. Trust in God—Christianity. 3. Rest—Religious aspects—Christianity. 4. Peace of mind—Religious aspects—
Christianity. I. Title.
    BV4509.5.S64 2010
    248.8'6—dc22
                                        2009042920
Printed in Canada
20 19 18 17 16 15 14 13   6 7 8 9 10

Married with three children, Bob played all of the roles typical of loving husbands and fathers. For his wife he was confidant, friend, and handyman. For his children, he was homework helper, chauffeur and cheerleader for sporting events, and a sympathetic ear to his daughters' occasional "boy troubles." His job was demanding. He was a mid-level manager for a company with tight resources and high expectations. Bob frequently felt the need to work overtime, doing things left undone by his employees. Involvement at church seemed like another endless "to do" list as he taught regularly, participated in various programs, and led a small-group Bible study.

A Very Tired Man

Over several months, Bob's stress levels had soared. As he accepted more and more responsibilities, he had less energy to bring to projects. Assignments were forgotten or neglected, people were disappointed, and Bob's anxiety and frustration grew. As it turns out, Bob's life was killing him—literally. One afternoon after a long day at work, Bob came home and had what seemed to be a heart attack. He was rushed to the hospital where he was diagnosed with an irregular heartbeat created by stress. The doctors recommended counseling. Bob had to find a way to slow down and learn to rest.

If Bob needed a reason to slow down, you would think he had one that no one could argue with. But someone did: Bob! Bob was in counseling because he didn't know how to stop. When asked to lay aside some responsibilities for his own good, Bob couldn't do it. In every area of his life, Bob would raise the same concerns: "But this is so important!" "But it's for the church!" "But it's for the kids!" "If *I* don't do it, who will?" "I would just feel too guilty." Bob was stuck on a treadmill of his own making.

Do you see yourself in Bob? Does your life feel like one long "to do" list? Do you find yourself saying yes to activities you don't have time for? Here's a tougher question: Are you, like Bob, driven as much by your own demands to perform as the requests of others? How many requests feel like demands only because of the way you perceive them? Short of having a heart attack, are you willing to slow down and rest?

A Command to Rest

There is one very important reason to slow down and rest. God commands it. In fact, resting is so important that it is one of the Ten Commandments. The fourth commandment reads, "Remember the Sabbath day by keeping it holy. Six days you shall labor and do all your work, but the seventh day is a Sabbath to the LORD your God" (Exodus 20:8–10). The word *Sabbath* comes from the Hebrew word for "ceasing" or "stopping." You may already be familiar with the idea of "Sabbath" from Sunday school or from hearing your parents or grandparents mention it, but have you ever wondered why God thinks that having a day of "stopping" is important enough to be one of the Ten Commandments?

The first instance of Sabbath in the Bible features God himself resting. In the opening chapter of Genesis, God creates everything that exists in six days: light and darkness, moon, sun, stars, land and sea, plants, animals, and humankind. Chapter 2 begins, "Thus the heavens and the earth were completed in all their vast array. By the seventh day God had finished the work he had been doing; so on the seventh day he rested from all his work. And God blessed the seventh day and made it holy, because on it he rested from all the work of creating that he had done" (Genesis 2:1–3).

In some ways this seems natural enough; after all, God had just created everything! Can you think of a task more deserving of rest? But notice *how* God created everything. Every act of creation required nothing more of God than a spoken word: "And God said. . . ." God isn't toiling in sweat and anguish—just the opposite. He created an ordered, obedient cosmos with nothing more than a few words from his lips. Not only was his labor effortless, it was also perfect. Every creative act began with a word and ended with the pronouncement, "And God saw that it was good."[1]

You may be so familiar with the story of creation that it no longer astounds you, but you can be sure that the original audience would have been amazed at the God of Genesis 1. The ancient world was completely unfamiliar with the notion of one God who created and ruled over all things. They were preoccupied with how *many* gods existed, who they were, and what their roles were. So the creation stories of other cultures were strikingly different from the one in Genesis. For instance, in the Babylonian creation story, the world is created through a battle between warring factions of gods. Marduk and Tiamat[2], champions representing each group, meet to do battle. Marduk ultimately prevails over Tiamat and uses her corpse to construct the cosmos. In victory, Marduk ascends to become the chief god and mankind is created out of the blood of one of Tiamat's vanquished accomplices to serve as slaves and do the dirty work the gods didn't want to do. What a contrast to Genesis! Babylon's gods battle for mastery, power, and control. They simply act like bigger versions of us. But the true God effortlessly creates and orders all things to be beautiful reflections of his glory and power. His day of rest is a demonstration of his absolute mastery and the happy obedience of his creation. God's rest isn't a picture of tiredness, but a display of his absolute sovereignty.

I Can't Manage My Checkbook in Six Days, Much Less the Universe

So what's the connection between God's day of rest and the rest we are commanded to observe? The Bible explains that God's people are to observe this rest in imitation of him. The fourth commandment is explained simply, "For in six days the LORD made the heavens and the earth, the sea, and all that is in them, but he rested on the seventh day. Therefore the LORD blessed the Sabbath day and made it holy" (Exodus 20:11). To hear this as a call to imitate God, you need to remember that God made humankind in his "image" (Genesis 1:27), that is, as his representatives on earth. As his image bearers we must serve God and live in a way that represents him well. In part, our Sabbath rest serves as a symbol of *his* Sabbath rest, an ongoing image of his power and glory.

You may be willing to tip your hat to God's power and glory, but his ability to manage all things effortlessly doesn't mean you're able to do the same. A day of rest may sound wonderful—until you realize how much farther behind you would fall if you lost that day to "catch up." But perhaps this points us to other reasons for observing the Sabbath. God's command to rest forces us to acknowledge that God isn't just in perfect control of *his* world, but *ours* as well. Resting means acknowledging that our world really belongs to him and we must entrust our well-being into his hands. If you rest for a day, will God keep your life from falling apart? In this sense, we can see how rest is an exercise in faith. Resting should be a way of living out the truth that our world belongs to God. We must trust that he is in loving control of it.

Take the Whole Year Off!

We've all had days when we've wished we could forget it all and take a personal day off from all responsibility.

Can you imagine calling the office and hearing your boss reply, "Take the *day* off? Why, I would actually like you to take the *whole year* off!" Assuming the shock didn't kill you, you would, no doubt, be elated. But you might also have some questions. First of all, who's going to pay for this time off? I mean, this is a paid vacation, right? Imagine that your boss's answer is, "No. I expect you to live on the money you earned last year." Suddenly, joy becomes anxiety. Could you make it for a year without income? Now it sounds more like a layoff than a vacation, doesn't it?

God's command to rest goes far beyond a command to set aside one day a week. In addition to a Sabbath day, God required Israel to set aside entire *years* as Sabbaths. Every seventh year was to be a Sabbath year in which no crops were to be planted or harvested. Leviticus 25:1–7 states,

> The LORD said to Moses on Mount Sinai,
> "Speak to the Israelites and say to them: 'When you enter the land I am going to give you, the

land itself must observe a Sabbath to the LORD.
For six years sow your fields, and for six years
prune your vineyards and gather their crops.
But in the seventh year the land is to have a
Sabbath of rest, a Sabbath to the LORD. Do not
sow your fields or prune your vineyards. Do not
reap what grows of itself or harvest the grapes
of your untended vines. The land is to have a
year of rest. Whatever the land yields during the
Sabbath year will be food for you—for yourself,
your manservant and maidservant, and the
hired worker and temporary resident who live
among you, as well as for your livestock and the
wild animals in your land. Whatever the land
produces may be eaten."

In other words, food may be taken directly from
the fields, but not planted or harvested in any system-
atic way. The Sabbath year is a time for the land to rest.
No doubt it benefits the soil to lie fallow so agricultural
nutrients can be restored, but if that were all God had

in mind, he certainly could have explained it that way. The fact that this is considered a Sabbath "to the LORD" alerts us to a deeper significance, which becomes clearer a few verses later when God anticipates Israel's reaction: "You may ask, 'What will we eat in the seventh year if we do not plant or harvest our crops?'" (Leviticus 25:20). It's easy to understand Israel's concern, isn't it? Is God asking us to starve?

Again, the Sabbath reveals our hearts. You have enough faith to rest for one day a week. Now rest for an entire year. Do you really trust God to care for you or, when push comes to shove, do you only trust God with life's incidentals? Do you recognize this world as God's or do you manage it as if it were your own? God doesn't leave us squirming in doubt. He graciously answers our questions before they come to our lips. "I will send you such a blessing in the sixth year that the land will yield enough for three years. While you plant during the eighth year, you will eat from the old crop and will continue to eat from it until the harvest of the ninth year comes in" (Leviticus 25:21–22). God's answer is, "Yes, I will care for you. Trust me." Isn't it wonderful that God doesn't respond, "How dare you doubt me?! Of course you won't obey, you horrid, faithless people!" Familiar with our frailty and doubts, God speaks kind, reassuring words while he asks us to take up the challenges of faith.

The Promises of Rest

But these Sabbaths were intended to do more than stretch our faith. They are also laced with sweet and comforting promises. In addition to weekly Sabbaths and Sabbath years, God commanded Israel to observe a "Jubilee" year every fiftieth year.[3] The Jubilee year points to even deeper truths embedded in "resting." The year would begin with the sound of a special trumpet sounded on the Day of Atonement, the day when the high priest would make sacrifices for the sins of all the people. God explains, "Consecrate the fiftieth year and proclaim liberty throughout the land to all its inhabitants" (Leviticus 25:10a). As in a normal Sabbath year, the land was to lie fallow. Crops could not be planted or harvested; only what was taken directly from the fields could be eaten (Leviticus 25:12).

But in addition the Israelites were to perform certain acts of "redemption."

First, God commanded that all Israelites were to return to their "family property." For the Israelites, the land wasn't simply real estate, but an important symbol of their relationship with God. When God began a special relationship with Israel through their forefather, Abraham, it was founded upon special promises of God's provision and care for them. In particular, God promised to bless Israel (and the whole world through them) by providing a place for them to live and increasing Abraham's descendants, developing them into a great nation that would inhabit the land.[4] The significance of receiving this land is heightened as we remember that Israel was enslaved in Egypt for hundreds of years before being led to the Promised Land. For Israel, living in the land was a sign of their relationship with God as their liberator and provider, and of their identity as his people. In the year of Jubilee, any land that had been sold was to go back to its original owner. Even apart from a year of Jubilee, an Israelite was always to have the option of "redeeming" or purchasing back his own land. If he could not redeem it, a relative was to do so. But in the year of Jubilee, regardless of a person's economic or social status, the land God had given to him would be returned. What a sweet promise to have a home, an inheritance, that couldn't be lost in a world of hardship and loss!

A second form of "redemption" had to do with servants and slaves. In general, Israelites were not to serve as slaves to one another. Even if for economic reasons an Israelite sold himself as a servant to another Israelite, it was only as a servant, not a slave. God states, "Because the Israelites are my servants, whom I brought out of Egypt, they must not be sold as slaves" (Leviticus 25:42). Occasionally an Israelite might become a slave to an alien or temporary resident within Israel. In such circumstances, either the man himself or one of his relatives had the right to purchase the Israelite out of slavery. In either case, as a servant to another Israelite or a slave to an alien, in the year of Jubilee servant and slave were to be freed to go back to their own land. "Even if he is not redeemed in any of these ways, he and his children are to be released in the Year of Jubilee, for the Israelites belong to me as servants. They are my servants, whom I brought out of Egypt. I am the LORD your God" (Leviticus 25:54–55). Sabbath as freedom from slavery doesn't just apply to the year of Jubilee. It is part of the weekly Sabbath as well. As the Ten Commandments are described in the Book of Deuteronomy, the Sabbath requires that all servants, even animals, are to observe this rest. "Remember that you were slaves in Egypt and that the LORD your God brought you out of there with a mighty hand and an outstretched arm. Therefore the LORD your God has commanded you to observe the Sabbath day" (Deuteronomy 5:15).

Don't let language about land, servants, and slaves distract you from the spiritual truths that apply to us as God's people today, no matter our cultural distance from Israel. What should these practices communicate to us? Simply put, God intends for us to be free. The focus and purpose of all of our labor, ultimately, is to serve him. No other person or institution may own our allegiance; any other allegiance is ultimately slavery.

God has freed us and will continue to free us. So these Sabbaths don't just point backward to the God of creation; they point to God as a deliverer as well. The year of Jubilee tells us that we can never lose our identity as God's freedmen and children. He is the One who delivers the enslaved and those he sets free are freed forever. In addition, the Sabbath and Jubilee tell us that God has a home for us. No matter what state we may find ourselves in, no matter how far from home we may feel, God has a place for us and he will always lead us there. God takes the enslaved and restores the created order of things by settling *his* people in *his* land.

Whom Do You Serve?

The Sabbath forces you to ask yourself important questions: Who or what controls your world? Whom or what do you serve? Do you live the life of a slave or the Lord's freedman? These are the kinds of questions Bob had to answer.

As he did, he learned some important things about himself. First, Bob's fear and anxiety revealed that in many ways he was a functional atheist. Bob believed

God existed, but in everyday life he lived as if *he* were God, the only one controlling his world. Under pressure, it didn't occur to Bob to ask for God's help or consider what God's purposes might be in the situation. Instead, Bob turned to himself. He tried to tough it out and hope things would get better. Even when Bob was conscious of God, he lived as if God were just another taskmaster, one more person who piled up responsibilities and measured his performance. Bob's unwillingness to rest showed that he didn't know God as the creator or liberator. On the one hand, Bob lived as if he alone ruled his world, and on the other hand, he lived as if God were a cruel master. Bob's refrain, "If I don't do it, who will?" was a prideful claim of self-sufficiency and a lament that God had placed too much on his shoulders.

Bob didn't just have a distorted view of God. He had a distorted view of others as well. As Bob looked at what was driving him, it became clear that much of what he did was based on what others thought and felt about him. Most of Bob's decisions were based on a set of unspoken concerns: *Will this make others happy or angry? Will they think I am a bad person if I say no?* Many of Bob's decisions were made more out of self-concern than concern for others. Decisions based on love are about the welfare of the other person, not what they will think of you. Serving others in hopes that they will like you is manipulation, not love, and it really can harm others. Sometimes Bob's service meant that others did not recognize or use their own abilities. In some cases, others avoided their responsibilities and relied on Bob instead of God. In effect, others were not growing because Bob was in the way! Like an overindulgent parent, Bob unwittingly handicapped the people he tried to love because his goal was their respect and approval, not their maturity. He allowed people to depend on him instead of God. Learning to rest would help Bob understand the needs of others and truly love them.

Bob's lack of Sabbath in his career exposed another issue. Bob said yes to all that was asked of him at work because he feared losing his job. This was similar to a fear of disappointing others or losing their respect, but for Bob the fear ran deeper. He feared losing his job because he was afraid he wouldn't find another. It's not that there weren't other management positions available, Bob simply felt incompetent to be a manager at all.

Bob's coworkers would tell you that he was an exceptional employee, but Bob's sense of inadequacy and fear drove him to take on too much responsibility. As hard as he worked, it was never enough to give him a sense of adequacy or to have any confidence in the affirmation he got at work. Bob's unwillingness to rest revealed a critical problem that was much more serious than a need for career counseling. Bob lived out of a sense of shame and inadequacy that had dogged him his entire life. In his heart, Bob considered himself a failure and a fraud. He lived as if it were just a matter of time until he was exposed as a failure at every level. His busyness was a failed attempt to address a problem with who he was as a person.

Jesus, Our Sabbath Rest

Does it seem strange to you that someone would try to cover up his inadequacy through his work? It's really not strange at all. The Bible tells us that it is one of our most basic inclinations as sinners. After Adam and Eve sinned, their very first acts were to cover themselves, to hide. They scrambled to cover their nakedness by sewing fig leaves together to hide from each other, and they hid in the garden to conceal themselves from God. Look beyond mere embarrassment over physical nakedness and see their profound shame. They had realized that they were morally filthy and there was nothing they could do to change it. Try to imagine that first horrifying moment of realizing that you are a sinner, deserving judgment, and living in the world of a holy and just God. Sinners have been looking for ways to cover themselves ever since. We will do anything we can to prove that we are making a contribution, that we are good, that we don't deserve God's disapproval. Like Adam and Eve, Bob wanted to hide from his deep sense of inadequacy. How much of *our* busyness is really an effort to prove our worth and escape the sense that there is something very wrong with us?

Complicating matters, when God confronted Adam and Eve, he cursed the very things in which men and women would seek to find their worth: he cursed their labor. He tells Eve, "I will greatly increase your pains in childbearing; with pain you will give birth to children" (Genesis 3:16). To Adam he says, "Cursed is the ground because of you; through painful toil you will eat of it all the days of your life. It will produce thorns and thistles for you, and you will eat the plants of the field. By the sweat of your brow you will eat your food until you return to the ground, since from it you were taken; for dust you are and to dust you will return" (Genesis 3:17b–19). The very things we would hope to give us meaning and worth have been cursed so that to be "fruitful" in them will require extreme effort. You may try to take pride in your work; you may try to find life and meaning in your children, but God isn't going to make it easy for you.

What's going on here? How can God argue for Sabbath rest on the one hand, but promise to frustrate our work on the other? The answer is that God wants us to find our rest in him, not in our own proud efforts. He won't allow us to successfully cover ourselves. He faithfully and lovingly steers us away from trusting in our own efforts so that we can find true rest in the work *he* has done.

The problem of being morally corrupt and sinful can't be solved by working harder. Who can do the work that won't just cover up the symptoms but really fix *who we are*?

Jesus has done the work required to clean up the filth in our hearts, to purify us and make us acceptable before God. To use the imagery of Sabbath, he has set us free from the slavery of sin. He has allowed us to return home.

It can be hard for us to accept and trust that Jesus has done our labor for us in a way we never could. There are few experiences in which the good efforts of another can make up for our own. For example, my son hates doing homework. My wife and I spend countless hours, not just helping him with his homework but urging him to press on, or even to just get started. Many times, the night before a paper or project is due, my son sits frustrated, almost in tears, because it's late and his work is not done. He isn't proud of the work he has done and, in his sleepy, angry stupor, there isn't much hope that his last hour or two of effort is going to make things better. These are moments when I would love to swoop in and apply my college education to his fifth-grade projects. It would be effortless. He would see me as his hero. He would get an A on his project. The tears would be wiped away and life would be so much easier—at least for a while. The problem is that while I can get an A for him on his project, it's not really his A—it's mine. The teacher might be foolish enough to give him credit for the work, but the ability would always be mine, never his. Sooner or later a day would arrive when he would be required to not only produce the grade but also demonstrate the ability and he would be worse off than ever.

Here's where we have to step away from our everyday experience and marvel at God's ability to rescue us in our inability. Jesus really did do our work for us in living a life perfect in every regard, keeping the whole of God's law, and paying the penalty for our countless violations. God has truly credited us with Jesus' perfection and success. We get Jesus' A+++. It's not fair, but that's the whole point: It is what the Bible calls "grace." Grace means we don't get what's fair or what we deserve; we get God's forgiveness and love instead. And not only are we credited with Jesus' perfection, we also, in time, gain the *ability* to do what is right. We aren't simply being let off the hook, but truly redeemed, or fixed, on the inside. By trusting in Jesus we are spiritually joined to him so that not only his credit, but also his very nature begins to take over ours. This is the amazing Sabbath we are to rest in. Not simply rest *from* our own efforts, but rest *in* Jesus' finished work for us.

The Book of Hebrews gives us a powerful picture of Jesus' work. In the Old Testament, Israel was required to offer regular sacrifices day after day and year after year to atone for their sins. These functions were carried out by priests at God's temple in Jerusalem. Hebrews points out that the fact these sacrifices had to be performed over and over again for hundreds of years shows that they were ineffective in truly removing sin. These sacrifices "repeated endlessly year after year" cannot "make perfect those who draw near to worship. If it could, would they not have stopped being offered? For the worshipers would have been cleansed once for all, and would no longer have felt guilty for their sins" (Hebrews 10:1–2).

Let the language of these tasks being "endless" and being required "year after year" make you tired. Feel the futility of it. Endless tasks that never get the job done. Sound familiar? But when Jesus comes, something amazing happens. Acting as our high priest, he makes a sacrifice of his own life and body that pays the debt once and for all. "Day after day every priest stands and performs his religious duties; again and again he offers the same sacrifices, which can never take away sins. But when this priest [Jesus] had offered for all time one sacrifice for sins, he sat down at the right hand of God. . . . by one sacrifice he has made perfect forever those who are being made holy" (Hebrews 10:11–14). The Old Testament sacrifices were intended, in part, to communicate a sense of futility. They were intended to drive home our need for a Redeemer, someone who could once and for all do what we are unable to do so we can truly rest. Jesus, unlike any other priest, completed his work and was able to sit down. Do you understand why it is important to have a Savior who is sitting? Like his Father in Genesis 1, Jesus sits because his labor for us is perfect and complete. In other words, "It was very good."

Because Jesus rests, you can rest. This is one reason many Christians choose to observe a Sabbath on Sundays, the first day of the week, rather than Saturdays, the last day of the week. Jesus' death and resurrection embody the promises of Sabbath. His work is perfect; we cannot and need not add to it. It is complete. He has paid for, or "redeemed" us from our sin. By trusting him and obeying his words and his Spirit within us, we are no longer slaves to our corrupted nature. We are free to be God's children. His resurrection is the promise of new life, a new start—a picture and promise of the new life we have now and will have forever when Jesus returns and we are resurrected as well.

Practical Strategies for Change

How Can I Begin to Rest?

Thoughtful and sincere Christians may disagree on what day and how Sabbath should be observed. But it is clear that God's people should be characterized by an attitude of Sabbath. We should know that we are different; we are not slaves to what enslaves others. We should express a peace that comes from belonging to the God who created and rules over all things for our good. Here are a few ways to build Sabbath into your life.

- Become a devoted admirer of Christ. The more deeply you appreciate and worship Christ in his perfection, the more confidence you will have in him. You will become less likely to trust in yourself. Rest must be rooted in faith. Don't try to simply plug rest into the problem. Be worshipful.

- Repent of the pride that says, "If I don't do it, who will?" We are a strange mixture of fear, pride, and rebellion. Fear and inadequacy are not the opposites of pride, but its fruit. Pride drives our attempts to fix problems ourselves rather than accepting what God has done. Pride tells us to trust in ourselves rather than God.

- Don't get in Jesus' way by being overly responsible. Allow others to experience their need for Christ. Know the difference between mercifully helping someone with his responsibility versus taking it on as your own.

- Be a student of your own heart. Countless motivations can drive us. What desires or fears keep you from resting? Here are a few to consider:

   o Do you live for the approval of others? Believing that your worth comes from others' approval is slavery. Do you fear their disapproval, bask in their praise, or both? If so, you make them your god and they

end up controlling your life. You will even-
tually experience this as slavery.

○ Do you enjoy the admiration of others
because you are known as a hard worker?
Does that badge keep you from facing
other deficits in your life?

○ Do you experience a low-grade anxiety
when you sit still? This might indicate that
you are avoiding seeing, knowing, or expe-
riencing something you need to face.

○ Do you need everything around you to
be neat, orderly, and in the right place?
Are you trying to find comfort by creating
your own ordered paradise in an otherwise
untidy world?

• Instead of being guilt-ridden about not having
regular quiet times, carve out daily times to "rest
in the Lord." Don't think of prayer simply as
presenting God with a list of requests, but as a
time to be quiet before him and thank him for
his work. Don't read the Bible as a task, but as a

time to be quiet and let God speak. Think about what it would look like to rest before him as an act of worship.

Fortunately, Bob has begun to learn how to rest. He has allowed God's simple command to "stop" to search his heart and direct him to God's power and love. In the past his efforts to rest were always accompanied by pangs of guilt and anxiety, but now he says that for the first time he is actually beginning to enjoy things in a new way. He hasn't become a lazy man, but a man whose work and rest are acts of faith and worship. Rest has become truly "restful" because he trusts in the perfect labor of Christ.

Endnotes

1 Genesis 1:10, 18, 21, 25, 31.
2 Interestingly, Tiamat is a goddess who represents the primordial sea. In contrast, Genesis 1 describes an unbounded primordial sea immediately subject to God's commands.
3 The year following a cycle of seven Sabbath years.
4 See Genesis 12:1–3; 15:18–21.

Simple, Quick, Biblical

Advice on Complicated Counseling Issues
for Pastors, Counselors, and Individuals

MINIBOOK
CATEGORIES

- Personal Change
- Marriage & Parenting
- Medical & Psychiatric Issues

- Women's Issues
- Singles
- Military

USE YOURSELF | GIVE TO A FRIEND | DISPLAY IN YOUR CHURCH OR MINISTRY

New Growth Press

Go to **www.newgrowthpress.com** or call **336.378.7775** to purchase individual minibooks or the entire collection. Durable acrylic display stands are also available to house the minibook collection.